I0007766

Mastering Azure Machine Learning:
From Fundamental to Deployment

Bimal P R Kujur

Preface

In a world where data has become the backbone of decision-making, artificial intelligence (AI) and machine learning (ML) are no longer optional for businesses and organizations—they are essential. Microsoft Azure Machine Learning (Azure ML) stands as a powerful platform that democratizes AI and ML, enabling individuals and organizations to build, train, deploy, and scale models efficiently. Whether you are an aspiring data scientist, an ML engineer, or a seasoned practitioner, the ability to harness Azure ML can set you apart as a leader in this transformative field.

Why This Book?

"Mastering Azure Machine Learning: From Fundamentals to Deployment" is designed to bridge the gap between foundational ML concepts and the complexities of deploying production-ready systems. While Azure ML's intuitive interface and robust APIs simplify many tasks, mastery of the platform requires an understanding of the underlying concepts, tools, and workflows. This book equips you with the skills and knowledge to navigate every stage of the machine learning lifecycle using Azure ML—from data preparation and model development to deployment, monitoring, and scaling.

Who Should Read This Book?

This book caters to a broad audience:

- Beginners: Individuals new to machine learning who want a structured guide to mastering Azure

ML's features while understanding fundamental ML concepts.

- Intermediate Practitioners: Those with some experience in ML who wish to deepen their knowledge of Azure ML's advanced capabilities, such as AutoML, distributed training, and pipeline orchestration.

- Professionals: Industry experts seeking insights into implementing scalable and efficient ML solutions in real-world scenarios.

Regardless of your starting point, this book emphasizes practical examples, clear explanations, and actionable insights to accelerate your Azure ML journey.

What You Will Learn

The book's modular structure ensures a comprehensive learning experience:

1. Foundations: Introduction to Azure ML, its architecture, and core capabilities.

2. Model Development: Hands-on guidance for building and training models, including data preprocessing, experimentation, and hyperparameter tuning.

3. AutoML and Responsible AI: Insights into automation, interpretability, and fairness to ensure ethical and impactful solutions.

4. Advanced Techniques: Distributed training, embedding models, and working with large language models.

5. Deployment: Real-world approaches to deploying, monitoring, and scaling ML systems on Azure.

6. Case Studies and Best Practices: Success stories across industries and actionable best practices for leveraging Azure ML effectively.

The Azure Ecosystem Advantage

The strength of Azure ML lies in its integration with Microsoft's robust cloud ecosystem. This book explores these synergies—from leveraging Azure DevOps for CI/CD pipelines to using Azure Synapse Analytics for data integration, and employing Azure Monitor for observability in deployed models. By mastering Azure ML, you gain access to a holistic set of tools and services that streamline the development and operationalization of machine learning.

A Practical and Forward-Looking Perspective

This book is more than a technical manual; it's a guide to navigating the dynamic field of AI and ML with Azure ML at its core. The rapid advancements in AI underscore the need for practitioners to remain adaptive and forward-thinking. As you move through this book, you will encounter both the technical nuances and strategic insights that position you to excel in AI-driven innovation.

Whether you aim to advance your career, drive transformative business outcomes, or explore the frontier of AI, this book is your comprehensive resource for mastering Azure ML.

Let's embark on this journey together to unlock the full potential of Azure Machine Learning!

Table of Contents

1. Getting Started with Azure Machine Learning

1.1 Setting Up an Azure Account

Azure Machine Learning is a cloud-based service by Microsoft, which means you need an Azure account to get started. Setting up an account is straightforward and can be done through the Azure portal. To begin, visit the Azure website, sign up for a new account, and select the appropriate subscription plan based on your needs. Once your account is set up, you can access the Azure portal, which serves as the central hub for all Azure services.

1.2 Navigating the Azure Portal

The Azure portal is a web-based application that provides a unified interface to manage Azure services. It is designed to be user-friendly, with a dashboard that can be customized to display your most frequently used resources and services. You will find navigation menus on the left side, and the main content area provides details about your selected services or resources.

Key Features of the Azure Portal:

- **Dashboard Customization**: Tailor the dashboard to show information relevant to your Azure ML projects.

- **Resource Management**: Access, create, and manage resources like virtual machines, databases, and machine learning workspaces.

- **Monitoring and Alerts**: Monitor resource performance and set up alerts to notify you of any issues.

1.3 Creating an Azure Machine Learning Workspace

An Azure Machine Learning Workspace is the cornerstone for building, training, and deploying machine learning models. It serves as a centralized place to manage all the machine learning resources needed for your project.

Steps to Create a Workspace:

1. Navigate to the Azure portal and search for "Machine Learning" in the search bar.

2. Select "Machine Learning" and click on "Create" to start the workspace creation process.

3. Fill in the necessary details such as the subscription, resource group, workspace name, and region.

4. Click "Review + create" and then "Create" to set up the workspace.

Once the workspace is created, it will appear in the list of resources. You can click on it to access the workspace dashboard, which provides an overview of all the machine learning assets like datasets, models, and endpoints.

1.4 Understanding Key Concepts and Terminology

To effectively use Azure Machine Learning, it's essential to understand several key concepts and terminologies:

- **Workspace**: The top-level resource that contains all your machine learning assets.

- **Dataset**: A collection of data used for training and evaluating models.

- **Compute Target**: The computational resources where the model training occurs, such as virtual machines or clusters.

- **Pipeline**: A series of steps in the machine learning process, from data preparation to model deployment.

- **Endpoint**: A web service that hosts the deployed model, allowing applications to consume predictions.

1.5 Initial Setup and Configuration

After creating your workspace, you need to configure it to start building models. This includes setting up compute resources, connecting to data sources, and installing necessary packages. Azure ML provides various options for compute resources, from simple virtual machines to powerful clusters that can handle large-scale data processing and model training tasks.

In this chapter, we covered the essential steps to get started with Azure Machine Learning, from setting up an Azure account to creating and configuring your workspace. In the next chapter, we will delve into data preparation, a crucial step in the machine learning workflow.

2. Data Preparation

2.1 Importing Data

Data is the backbone of any machine learning project, and Azure Machine Learning provides multiple ways to import data from different sources. Whether your data resides in cloud storage services like Azure Blob Storage, databases, or local files, Azure ML has tools to facilitate seamless data importation.

Data Sources and Connectivity

- **Azure Blob Storage**: Azure's object storage solution for the cloud, ideal for storing large amounts of unstructured data.

- **SQL Databases**: Azure SQL Database and other SQL-based databases can be connected to Azure ML for structured data access.

- **Local Files**: For smaller datasets or initial experiments, you can upload files directly from your local machine.

2.2 Data Cleaning and Transformation

Raw data often requires cleaning and transformation before it can be used for model training. Azure ML provides tools to handle missing values, correct data inconsistencies, and transform data into a suitable format for machine learning.

Steps in Data Cleaning:

1. **Handling Missing Values**: Use techniques like mean imputation or removing rows/columns with missing data.

2. **Correcting Data Types**: Ensure that each feature in the dataset has the correct data type (e.g., numeric, categorical).

3. **Removing Outliers**: Identify and remove outliers that can skew the results of your machine learning model.

2.3 Feature Engineering

Feature engineering involves creating new features from the existing data to improve the model's predictive power. It is one of the most critical steps in building an effective machine learning model.

Techniques in Feature Engineering:

- **Feature Creation**: Generate new features by combining or transforming existing ones.

- **Feature Selection**: Use statistical methods to select the most relevant features for the model.

- **Normalization and Scaling**: Standardize data to ensure that features contribute equally to the model's predictions.

Azure ML offers built-in modules and custom scripts to assist with feature engineering tasks, enabling you to fine-tune the dataset for optimal model performance.

In this chapter, we have explored the data preparation process, covering data import, cleaning, and feature engineering. In the next chapter, we will move on to building machine learning models using Azure Machine Learning.

3. Building Machine Learning Models with Azure

In this chapter, we will explore the process of building machine learning models using Microsoft Azure. Azure provides a comprehensive suite of tools and services that streamline the development, training, and deployment of machine learning models. Whether you are a data scientist, a machine learning engineer, or a software developer, Azure offers scalable and flexible solutions to support your machine learning projects.

Overview of Azure Machine Learning

Azure Machine Learning (Azure ML) is a cloud-based service that facilitates the end-to-end machine learning lifecycle. It supports various stages, including data preparation, model training, model evaluation, and deployment. Azure ML integrates with other Azure services, such as Azure Data Lake, Azure Databricks, and Azure Kubernetes Service, to provide a robust ecosystem for machine learning development.

Key Features of Azure ML:

- **Automated Machine Learning (AutoML):** Automates the process of selecting the best machine learning algorithms and hyperparameters.

- **Experimentation**: Allows for tracking and managing experiments to compare different model versions and configurations.

- **Model Management**: Supports versioning, registration, and deployment of machine learning models.

- **Integration with Azure DevOps**: Enables CI/CD pipelines for machine learning models.

- **Security and Compliance**: Ensures data security and regulatory compliance through Azure's security features.

Setting Up Azure ML Workspace

Before building machine learning models, you need to set up an Azure ML workspace. This workspace acts as a central hub for all machine learning activities.

Steps to Set Up Azure ML Workspace:

1. **Sign in to Azure Portal**: Navigate to the Azure Portal.

2. **Create a Resource Group**: Organize your Azure resources by creating a new resource group or using an existing one.

3. **Create an Azure ML Workspace**: Search for "Azure Machine Learning" in the marketplace and create a new workspace. Provide the necessary details, such as subscription, resource group, and workspace name.

4. **Configure Workspace Settings**: Customize settings like networking, encryption, and diagnostic logs as per your requirements.

Once the workspace is created, you can access it through the Azure Portal, Azure ML Studio, or Azure CLI.

Data Preparation

Data preparation is a crucial step in building machine learning models. Azure ML offers tools to facilitate data ingestion, cleaning, and transformation.

Azure Data Preparation Tools:

- **Azure Data Factory**: Orchestrates data workflows and integrates with various data sources.

- **Azure Databricks**: Provides an Apache Spark-based platform for big data processing and machine learning.

- **Data Prep SDK**: Offers Python-based libraries for data manipulation and transformation.

Example Workflow:

1. **Ingest Data**: Use Azure Data Factory to import data from sources like SQL databases, blob storage, or APIs.

2. **Clean and Transform**: Apply data cleaning and transformation techniques using Azure Databricks or Data Prep SDK.

3. **Feature Engineering**: Create new features that enhance the predictive power of the models.

4. **Store Processed Data**: Save the prepared data in Azure Blob Storage or Azure Data Lake for easy access during model training.

Building and Training Models

Azure ML supports various ways to build and train machine learning models, including using Jupyter notebooks, AutoML, and the Designer interface.

Jupyter Notebooks:

Jupyter notebooks are commonly used for interactive data analysis and model development. Azure ML provides a cloud-hosted Jupyter environment with pre-installed machine learning libraries.

Automated Machine Learning (AutoML):

AutoML automates the model selection and hyperparameter tuning process. You need to specify the dataset and target column, and AutoML will handle the rest.

Azure ML Designer:

The Designer interface offers a drag-and-drop experience for building machine learning workflows. It is ideal for users who prefer a visual approach over coding.

Training Models:

1. **Create an Experiment**: Initiate a new experiment in Azure ML to track the training runs.

2. **Configure Compute Target**: Choose a compute target, such as a local machine, Azure VM, or Azure ML Compute cluster, to run the training job.

3. **Run Training Script**: Execute your training script in the experiment. Use libraries like TensorFlow, PyTorch, or Scikit-learn as needed.

4. **Monitor Training**: Track metrics like accuracy, loss, and training duration through Azure ML's monitoring tools.

Model Evaluation and Tuning

After training, it's essential to evaluate the model's performance and fine-tune it to achieve the best results.

Evaluation Metrics:

- **Accuracy**: Measures the percentage of correct predictions.

- **Precision and Recall**: Evaluate the relevance and completeness of the predictions.

- **F1 Score**: Balances precision and recall to provide a single metric.

- **AUC-ROC**: Analyzes the trade-off between true positive rate and false positive rate.

Hyperparameter Tuning:

Azure ML supports hyperparameter tuning through grid search, random search, and Bayesian optimization. This process helps in finding the optimal set of hyperparameters for the model.

Model Deployment

Once a model is trained and evaluated, the next step is to deploy it for use in production environments.

Deployment Options:

- **Azure Kubernetes Service (AKS)**: Deploy scalable machine learning models as REST APIs using AKS.

- **Azure Functions**: Serve models with serverless computing using Azure Functions.

- **Azure IoT Edge**: Deploy models to edge devices for real-time inference.

Steps for Deployment:

1. **Register Model**: Save the trained model in the Azure ML model registry.

2. **Create Inference Configuration**: Define the environment and dependencies required for the model.

3. **Deploy Service**: Use Azure ML SDK or Azure Portal to deploy the model as a web service.

4. **Monitor and Maintain**: Continuously monitor the deployed model for performance and update it as needed.

4. Hyperparameter Tuning with Azure Machine Learning

Hyperparameter tuning is a critical step in building effective machine learning models. The performance of a model often depends on the choice of hyperparameters, which are settings used to control the training process. In this chapter, we will explore how Azure Machine Learning (Azure ML) provides robust tools and services to automate and optimize hyperparameter tuning, enabling data scientists and machine learning engineers to achieve the best possible model performance.

Overview of Hyperparameter Tuning

Hyperparameters are parameters that are not learned from the data but are set prior to the training process. Examples include learning rate, batch size, number of hidden layers, and number of neurons in each layer. Tuning these hyperparameters is essential to improve model accuracy and generalization.

Common Hyperparameters:

- **Learning Rate**: Controls how much the model weights are updated during training.

- **Batch Size**: Determines the number of training examples utilized in one iteration.

- **Number of Epochs**: Defines the number of complete passes through the training dataset.

- **Regularization Parameters**: Prevent overfitting by adding a penalty to the loss function.

Hyperparameter Tuning Strategies

There are several strategies for hyperparameter tuning, including manual search, grid search, random search, and more advanced techniques like Bayesian optimization. Azure ML supports these strategies and provides additional capabilities to streamline the tuning process.

Grid Search:

Grid search is a brute-force approach where all possible combinations of hyperparameter values are tried. While exhaustive, it can be computationally expensive and time-consuming.

Random Search:

Random search selects random combinations of hyperparameters, which often finds good combinations faster than grid search due to its ability to explore a larger space in fewer iterations.

Bayesian Optimization:

Bayesian optimization uses probabilistic models to select the most promising hyperparameters, balancing exploration and exploitation. It is more efficient than grid or random search and is particularly useful for high-dimensional search spaces.

Hyperparameter Tuning with Azure ML

Azure ML simplifies hyperparameter tuning through its built-in tools and services, allowing users to define and manage tuning experiments efficiently.

Key Features:

- **HyperDrive**: Azure ML's hyperparameter tuning service that supports various search strategies, early stopping, and distributed training.

- **Experiment Tracking**: Automatically tracks all tuning runs, including hyperparameter values, metrics, and logs.

- **Integration with Compute Targets**: Leverages Azure compute resources like Azure ML Compute, Azure Kubernetes Service (AKS), and more.

Using HyperDrive for Hyperparameter Tuning

HyperDrive is a powerful tool in Azure ML for automating hyperparameter tuning. It supports multiple search strategies and provides flexibility in configuring tuning jobs.

Steps to Use HyperDrive:

1. **Define the Search Space**: Specify the range or set of values for each hyperparameter to be tuned.

2. **Choose a Search Strategy**: Select from grid search, random search, or Bayesian optimization.

3. **Configure Early Stopping**: Set criteria to terminate underperforming runs early, saving time and resources.

4. **Submit the HyperDrive Run**: Launch the tuning experiment and monitor its progress through Azure ML's dashboard or SDK.

Example:

```
from            azureml.train.hyperdrive            import
RandomParameterSampling, BanditPolicy

from azureml.train.hyperdrive import HyperDriveConfig,
PrimaryMetricGoal

from azureml.train.hyperdrive import choice, loguniform


# Define parameter sampling

param_sampling = RandomParameterSampling({

    'learning_rate': loguniform(-6, -1),

    'batch_size': choice(16, 32, 64, 128)

})


# Define early stopping policy

early_stopping_policy                                =
BanditPolicy(evaluation_interval=2, slack_factor=0.1)
```

```
# Configure HyperDrive

hyperdrive_config = HyperDriveConfig(

    run_config=your_run_config,

    hyperparameter_sampling=param_sampling,

    policy=early_stopping_policy,

    primary_metric_name='accuracy',

    primary_metric_goal=PrimaryMetricGoal.MAXIMIZE,

    max_total_runs=20,

    max_concurrent_runs=4

)


# Submit the HyperDrive run

hyperdrive_run = experiment.submit(hyperdrive_config)
```

Monitoring and Analyzing Results

Azure ML provides tools to monitor and analyze the results of hyperparameter tuning experiments. The Azure ML dashboard displays the performance of each run, allowing you to compare different hyperparameter configurations and identify the best-performing model.

Key Metrics to Monitor:

- **Primary Metric**: The main metric used to evaluate model performance, such as accuracy, F1 score, or AUC-ROC.

- **Secondary Metrics**: Additional metrics that provide insights into other aspects of the model's performance.

- **Resource Usage**: Tracks the compute resources consumed during the tuning process.

Analyzing Results:

- Use the Azure ML SDK or portal to visualize the performance of different hyperparameter configurations.

- Select the best model based on the primary metric and register it for deployment.

Best Practices for Hyperparameter Tuning

To get the most out of hyperparameter tuning with Azure ML, consider the following best practices:

- **Start with Random Search**: Use random search for an initial exploration of the hyperparameter space.

- **Leverage Early Stopping**: Configure early stopping policies to terminate poor-performing runs early.

- **Use Bayesian Optimization for Refinement**: After initial exploration, use Bayesian optimization to fine-tune the hyperparameters.

- **Monitor Resource Usage**: Keep an eye on resource usage to optimize cost and performance.

- **Document Experiments**: Maintain detailed documentation of the tuning process and results for future reference.

5. Model Deployment with Azure Machine Learning

Deploying machine learning models is a crucial step in bringing your trained models into production environments. Azure Machine Learning (Azure ML) provides comprehensive services to streamline the deployment process, enabling you to serve your models efficiently and securely. In this chapter, we will explore how to deploy machine learning models using Azure ML, covering different deployment strategies, tools, and best practices.

Overview of Model Deployment

Model deployment refers to the process of making a machine learning model available for use in a production environment. This involves packaging the model, setting up the necessary infrastructure, and exposing the model through APIs or other interfaces.

Key Concepts:

- Model Packaging: Wrapping the trained model with necessary dependencies.
- Infrastructure Setup: Configuring servers or cloud services to host the model.
- Serving the Model: Providing interfaces (e.g., REST APIs) to interact with the model.
- Monitoring: Tracking the performance and usage of the deployed model.

Azure ML Deployment Options:

Azure ML supports multiple deployment options tailored to different use cases and environments.

Azure Kubernetes Service (AKS):

AKS is a managed Kubernetes service that allows for scalable deployment of containerized applications, including machine learning models.

- Advantages: Scalability, high availability, and integration with Azure services.
- Use Cases: Suitable for large-scale deployments requiring high availability and fault tolerance.

Azure Container Instances (ACI):

ACI provides a fast and simple way to deploy containerized applications without managing complex infrastructure.

- Advantages: Simplicity, quick setup, and cost-effectiveness.
- Use Cases: Ideal for development, testing, or low-traffic applications.

Azure Functions:

Azure Functions is a serverless computing service that runs code in response to events. It can be used to deploy lightweight models with minimal infrastructure management.

- Advantages: Serverless, automatic scaling, and cost-effective for sporadic workloads.

- Use Cases: Suitable for event-driven applications and low-latency use cases.

Azure IoT Edge:

Azure IoT Edge extends cloud intelligence to edge devices by deploying and running machine learning models locally.

- Advantages: Low latency, offline capabilities, and real-time processing.
- Use Cases: Ideal for scenarios requiring real-time predictions on edge devices.

Steps for Deploying Models in Azure ML

Deploying a model in Azure ML involves several steps, from registering the model to creating and deploying an inference configuration.

Step 1: Model Registration

Before deployment, the trained model must be registered in the Azure ML workspace. This step ensures that the model is versioned and stored securely.

Example:

from azureml.core.model import Model

Register the model

model = Model.register(workspace=workspace,

```
model_name='my_model',

model_path='outputs/my_model.pkl')
```

Step 2: Create Inference Configuration

The inference configuration defines the environment and dependencies required for the model to run.

Example:

```
from azureml.core.environment import Environment

from azureml.core.model import InferenceConfig


# Define the environment

env = Environment(name='my_env')

env.docker.enabled = True

env.python.conda_dependencies.add_pip_package('scikit-learn')


# Define the inference configuration

inference_config = InferenceConfig(entry_script='score.py', environment=env)
```

Step 3: Deploy the Model

The deployment configuration specifies the target deployment service and settings such as CPU and memory requirements.

Example for ACI Deployment:

```
from azureml.core.webservice import AciWebservice, Webservice


# Define the deployment configuration

deployment_config = AciWebservice.deploy_configuration(cpu_cores=1, memory_gb=1)


# Deploy the model

service = Model.deploy(workspace=workspace,

          name='my-service',

          models=[model],

          inference_config=inference_config,

          deployment_config=deployment_config)


service.wait_for_deployment(show_output=True)
```

Step 4: Test the Deployment

Once the model is deployed, you can test the service by sending HTTP requests with input data.

Example:

import requests

Define the endpoint URL

scoring_uri = service.scoring_uri

Send a test request

data = {'data': [[1, 2, 3, 4]]}

response = requests.post(scoring_uri, json=data)

print(response.json())

Monitoring and Managing Deployed Models

After deployment, it's crucial to monitor the performance and health of your model. Azure ML provides tools to manage deployed services, track usage, and handle updates.

Monitoring Tools:

- Azure ML Dashboard: Offers a comprehensive view of deployed models, including usage metrics and logs.
- Application Insights: Integrates with Azure ML to provide detailed telemetry data, such as request latency and error rates.

Managing Updates:

- Model Redeployment: Update models by redeploying new versions without downtime.
- A/B Testing: Deploy multiple versions of a model to test and compare performance before fully rolling out updates.

6. Advanced Topics in Azure Machine Learning

As machine learning matures, the need for advanced capabilities and sophisticated tools becomes crucial for building, managing, and deploying models at scale. Azure Machine Learning (Azure ML) provides a suite of advanced features to address these challenges, from distributed training to model interpretability and compliance. In this chapter, we delve into these advanced topics, empowering you to harness the full potential of Azure ML.

Distributed Training

Training large-scale machine learning models often requires significant computational resources. Distributed training allows the training process to be divided across multiple machines, accelerating the process and enabling the handling of larger datasets.

Types of Distributed Training:

- Data Parallelism: Splits data across multiple nodes, each training a model copy on its subset of data.
- Model Parallelism: Splits the model itself across multiple nodes, each handling a portion of the model's parameters.

Azure ML and Distributed Training:

Azure ML supports distributed training through integration with frameworks like TensorFlow, PyTorch, and MPI (Message Passing Interface).

Example for Distributed Training with TensorFlow:

```
from azureml.core import ScriptRunConfig, Environment

from azureml.core.runconfig import MpiConfiguration


# Define environment

env = Environment.from_conda_specification(name='tf-env', file_path='environment.yml')


# Configure MPI-based distributed training

mpi_config = MpiConfiguration(node_count=4, process_count_per_node=2)


# Create a ScriptRunConfig

src = ScriptRunConfig(source_directory='.',

            script='train.py',

            compute_target='cluster',
```

```
        environment=env,

        distributed_job_config=mpi_config)
```

```
# Submit the job

experiment.submit(src)
```

Model Interpretability

Interpretability is critical for understanding model behavior, especially in sensitive applications like healthcare and finance. Azure ML offers tools to explain model predictions, making machine learning more transparent and trustworthy.

Azure ML Interpretability Features:

- SHAP (SHapley Additive exPlanations): Explains the output of any machine learning model using game theory.
- LIME (Local Interpretable Model-agnostic Explanations): Provides local explanations for individual predictions.
- Azure ML SDK: Integrates interpretability tools directly into the machine learning workflow.

Example of Using SHAP with Azure ML:

```
from azureml.interpret import ExplanationClient

from interpret.ext.azureml.engine.explanation_client import ExplanationClient
```

```python
# Load the model and data

model = load_model('my_model.pkl')

data = load_data('test_data.csv')


# Generate SHAP explanations

explainer = shap.Explainer(model.predict, data)

shap_values = explainer(data)


# Visualize the SHAP values

shap.summary_plot(shap_values, data)


# Log explanations to Azure ML

client = ExplanationClient.from_run(run)

client.upload_model_explanation(shap_values)
```

Automated Machine Learning (AutoML)

AutoML simplifies the process of selecting the best algorithms and hyperparameters for a given dataset. It automates model selection, feature engineering, and hyperparameter tuning, accelerating the model development process.

Key Features of AutoML in Azure ML:

- Algorithm Selection: Automatically selects the best algorithm for the problem.
- Feature Engineering: Applies transformations to improve model performance.
- Hyperparameter Optimization: Tunes hyperparameters to find the optimal configuration.

Example of Using AutoML:

```
from azureml.train.automl import AutoMLConfig
```

```
# Configure AutoML

auto_ml_config = AutoMLConfig(

    task='classification',

    primary_metric='accuracy',

    experiment_timeout_minutes=30,

    training_data=training_data,

    label_column_name='target',
```

```
    n_cross_validations=5

)
```

```python
# Submit the AutoML experiment

experiment = Experiment(workspace, 'automl-experiment')

run = experiment.submit(auto_ml_config)
```

```python
# Monitor the run

run.wait_for_completion()
```

Compliance and Security

Ensuring compliance with data protection regulations and maintaining security is paramount in machine learning applications. Azure ML provides robust features to address these concerns.

Compliance Features:

- Data Encryption: Supports encryption at rest and in transit.
- Access Control: Integrates with Azure Active Directory for managing user access.
- Audit Logs: Tracks actions performed on resources for compliance and troubleshooting.

Security Best Practices:

- Use Managed Identities: Securely connect to Azure resources without managing credentials.
- Network Isolation: Deploy resources within a virtual network to restrict access.
- Regularly Update Environments: Keep environments up-to-date with the latest security patches.

Real-time Inference:

Real-time inference allows models to make predictions instantly in response to incoming data. Azure ML supports real-time inference through managed endpoints and integration with Azure services.

Deploying for Real-time Inference:

- Azure Kubernetes Service (AKS): Deploy scalable, low-latency APIs for real-time predictions.
- Azure Functions: Use serverless functions for lightweight, event-driven inference.

Example for Real-time Inference with AKS:

```
from azureml.core.webservice import AksWebservice, Webservice
```

```
# Define the AKS configuration
```

```python
aks_config                                                    =
AksWebservice.deploy_configuration(cpu_cores=2,
memory_gb=4)


# Deploy the model

service = Model.deploy(workspace=workspace,

                name='real-time-service',

                models=[model],

                inference_config=inference_config,

                deployment_config=aks_config)


service.wait_for_deployment(show_output=True)


# Test the service

import requests

response = requests.post(service.scoring_uri, json=data)

print(response.json())
```

7. Linear Regression with Azure Machine Learning

Linear regression is one of the most fundamental techniques in the field of machine learning. It is used for predicting a continuous target variable based on one or more predictor variables. In this chapter, we will explore how to implement and deploy a linear regression model using Azure Machine Learning (Azure ML). We will cover data preparation, model training, evaluation, and deployment, highlighting how Azure ML simplifies these processes.

Introduction to Linear Regression

Linear regression models the relationship between a dependent variable and one or more independent variables using a linear equation. The general form of a linear regression model is:

$$y=\beta_0+\beta_1x_1+\beta_2x_2+...+\beta_nx_n+\epsilon$$

Where:

- y is the dependent variable (target).

- $x_1,x_2,...,x_n$ are the independent variables (features).

- $\beta_0,\beta_1,...,\beta_n$ are the coefficients.

- ϵ is the error term.

Applications of Linear Regression:

- Predicting sales, prices, or other continuous outcomes.

- Analyzing relationships between variables.

- Forecasting trends.

Data Preparation

Before building a linear regression model, we need to prepare the data. This involves data collection, cleaning, and feature engineering.

Steps in Data Preparation:

1. **Data Collection**: Gather the dataset that contains the target variable and predictor variables.

2. **Data Cleaning**: Handle missing values, remove duplicates, and correct inconsistencies.

3. **Feature Engineering**: Transform raw data into meaningful features. This may include scaling, encoding categorical variables, and generating polynomial features for better model performance.

Example Data Preparation:

```
import pandas as pd

from sklearn.model_selection import train_test_split

from sklearn.preprocessing import StandardScaler


# Load the dataset
```

```python
data = pd.read_csv('housing.csv')

# Handle missing values
data.fillna(data.mean(), inplace=True)

# Split the dataset into features and target
X = data[['feature1', 'feature2', 'feature3']]
y = data['price']

# Split into training and test sets
X_train, X_test, y_train, y_test = train_test_split(X, y,
test_size=0.2, random_state=42)

# Standardize features
scaler = StandardScaler()
X_train_scaled = scaler.fit_transform(X_train)
X_test_scaled = scaler.transform(X_test)
```

Model Training

Training a linear regression model involves finding the optimal coefficients that minimize the difference between the predicted and actual values.

Using Scikit-learn for Linear Regression:

Azure ML supports popular machine learning libraries such as Scikit-learn, which provides an easy-to-use API for linear regression.

Example of Model Training:

```
from sklearn.linear_model import LinearRegression
```

```
# Initialize the model
model = LinearRegression()
```

```
# Train the model
model.fit(X_train_scaled, y_train)
```

Model Evaluation

Evaluating the performance of the model is crucial to ensure it makes accurate predictions on new data. Common metrics for linear regression include Mean Squared Error (MSE), Root Mean Squared Error (RMSE), and R-squared (R^2) score.

Example of Model Evaluation:

```
from sklearn.metrics import mean_squared_error, r2_score
```

```
# Make predictions
y_pred = model.predict(X_test_scaled)
```

```
# Calculate evaluation metrics

mse = mean_squared_error(y_test, y_pred)

rmse=mean_squared_error(y_test,          y_pred,
squared=False)

r2 = r2_score(y_test, y_pred)


print(f'MSE: {mse}, RMSE: {rmse}, R^2: {r2}')
```

Model Deployment with Azure ML

Once the model is trained and evaluated, the next step is to deploy it using Azure ML. This allows the model to be accessed and used for predictions via an API endpoint.

Steps for Deployment:

1. **Model Registration**: Save the trained model in the Azure ML workspace.

2. **Inference Configuration**: Define the environment and scoring script for the model.

3. **Deployment**: Deploy the model to a compute target such as Azure Container Instances (ACI) or Azure Kubernetes Service (AKS).

Example of Model Deployment:

```
from azureml.core import Workspace, Model

from azureml.core.webservice import AciWebservice, Webservice
```

```python
from azureml.core.model import InferenceConfig

# Connect to the workspace
ws = Workspace.from_config()

# Register the model
model = Model.register(workspace=ws,
                model_name='linear_regression_model',

model_path='outputs/linear_regression_model.pkl')

# Define the inference configuration
inference_config                                    =
InferenceConfig(entry_script='score.py',
environment=env)

# Define the deployment configuration
deployment_config                                   =
AciWebservice.deploy_configuration(cpu_cores=1,
memory_gb=1)

# Deploy the model
service = Model.deploy(workspace=ws,
```

```
name='linear-regression-service',

models=[model],

inference_config=inference_config,

deployment_config=deployment_config)
```

```
service.wait_for_deployment(show_output=True)
```

Monitoring and Managing the Deployed Model

After deployment, it is essential to monitor the model's performance and usage. Azure ML provides tools to track the deployed model's health and update it as needed.

Monitoring Tools:

- **Azure ML Dashboard**: Visualize performance metrics and logs.

- **Application Insights**: Provides detailed telemetry data, such as response times and error rates.

8. Logistic Regression with Azure Machine Learning

Logistic regression is a fundamental classification technique used in machine learning for predicting binary outcomes. Unlike linear regression, which predicts continuous values, logistic regression predicts probabilities that map to discrete classes. In this chapter, we will explore how to implement and deploy a logistic regression model using Azure Machine Learning (Azure ML). We'll cover data preparation, model training, evaluation, and deployment.

Introduction to Logistic Regression

Logistic regression models the probability that a given input belongs to a particular category. The logistic function (also known as the sigmoid function) is used to map the output of the linear equation to a probability between 0 and 1.

Logistic Function (Sigmoid Function)

The logistic regression model uses the sigmoid function to map predicted values to probabilities:

$$\sigma(z) = \frac{1}{1 + e^{-z}}$$

where:

- $\sigma(z)$ is the output probability

- z is the linear combination of input variables:

$$z = \beta_0 + \beta_1 x_1 + \beta_2 x_2 + \ldots + \beta_n x_n$$

- β_0 is the intercept
- $\beta_1, \beta_2, \ldots, \beta_n$ are the coefficients
- $x_1, x_2, \ldots, x_n$ are the independent variables

Applications of Logistic Regression:

- Spam detection
- Credit scoring
- Disease diagnosis
- Customer churn prediction

Data Preparation

Preparing the data is a crucial step before training the model. This includes data cleaning, transformation, and splitting into training and testing sets.

Steps in Data Preparation:

1. **Data Collection**: Obtain the dataset containing the features and the binary target variable.

2. **Data Cleaning**: Handle missing values, remove outliers, and standardize data if necessary.

3. **Feature Engineering**: Create new features, encode categorical variables, and scale numerical features.

Example Data Preparation:

```python
import pandas as pd

from sklearn.model_selection import train_test_split

from sklearn.preprocessing import StandardScaler


# Load the dataset
data = pd.read_csv('customer_data.csv')


# Handle missing values
data.fillna(data.mean(), inplace=True)


# Split the dataset into features and target
X = data[['age', 'income', 'credit_score']]
y = data['churn']


# Split into training and test sets
X_train, X_test, y_train, y_test = train_test_split(X, y, test_size=0.2, random_state=42)
```

```
# Standardize features

scaler = StandardScaler()

X_train_scaled = scaler.fit_transform(X_train)

X_test_scaled = scaler.transform(X_test)
```

Model Training

Training the logistic regression model involves finding the optimal coefficients that minimize the error between predicted and actual outcomes.

Using Scikit-learn for Logistic Regression:

Azure ML supports Scikit-learn, a popular machine learning library that includes logistic regression.

Example of Model Training:

```
from sklearn.linear_model import LogisticRegression


# Initialize the model

model = LogisticRegression()


# Train the model

model.fit(X_train_scaled, y_train)
```

Model Evaluation

Evaluating the logistic regression model's performance ensures it generalizes well to new data. Common metrics include Accuracy, Precision, Recall, and F1 Score.

Example of Model Evaluation:

```
from sklearn.metrics import accuracy_score,
precision_score, recall_score, f1_score


# Make predictions
y_pred = model.predict(X_test_scaled)


# Calculate evaluation metrics
accuracy = accuracy_score(y_test, y_pred)
precision = precision_score(y_test, y_pred)
recall = recall_score(y_test, y_pred)
f1 = f1_score(y_test, y_pred)


print(f'Accuracy: {accuracy}, Precision: {precision},
Recall: {recall}, F1 Score: {f1}')
```

Model Deployment with Azure ML

Deploying the logistic regression model using Azure ML allows it to be accessed via an API endpoint for making predictions in real-time.

Steps for Deployment:

1. **Model Registration**: Register the trained model in Azure ML workspace.

2. **Inference Configuration**: Define the environment and scoring script for the model.

3. **Deployment**: Deploy the model to a compute target such as Azure Container Instances (ACI) or Azure Kubernetes Service (AKS).

Example of Model Deployment:

```
from azureml.core import Workspace, Model

from azureml.core.webservice import AciWebservice, Webservice

from azureml.core.model import InferenceConfig


# Connect to the workspace
ws = Workspace.from_config()


# Register the model
model = Model.register(workspace=ws,

                model_name='logistic_regression_model',


model_path='outputs/logistic_regression_model.pkl')


# Define the inference configuration
```

```python
inference_config                                    =
InferenceConfig(entry_script='score.py',
environment=env)


# Define the deployment configuration

deployment_config                                   =
AciWebservice.deploy_configuration(cpu_cores=1,
memory_gb=1)


# Deploy the model

service = Model.deploy(workspace=ws,

                name='logistic-regression-service',

                models=[model],

                inference_config=inference_config,

                deployment_config=deployment_config)


service.wait_for_deployment(show_output=True)
```

Monitoring and Managing the Deployed Model

Monitoring the deployed model ensures it continues to perform well in production. Azure ML provides tools to manage deployed models and track performance.

Monitoring Tools:

- **Azure ML Dashboard**: Provides insights into model performance and usage.

- **Application Insights**: Offers detailed telemetry data, such as response times and errors.

9. Classification with Azure Machine Learning

Classification is a core task in machine learning where the goal is to predict the category or class of a given data point. This chapter will explore how to build and deploy classification models using Azure Machine Learning (Azure ML). We will cover the entire workflow, from data preparation to model training, evaluation, and deployment.

Introduction to Classification

Classification involves predicting discrete class labels for instances based on their features. It is widely used in various domains such as email spam detection, image recognition, and medical diagnosis.

Types of Classification:

- **Binary Classification**: Classifies data into two categories (e.g., spam or not spam).

- **Multiclass Classification**: Classifies data into more than two categories (e.g., types of flowers).

Data Preparation

Effective data preparation is essential for building robust classification models. This process includes gathering, cleaning, and transforming the data into a suitable format for model training.

Steps in Data Preparation:

1. **Data Collection**: Acquire datasets with features and corresponding class labels.

2. **Data Cleaning**: Handle missing values, remove duplicates, and correct inconsistencies.

3. **Feature Engineering**: Create meaningful features, encode categorical variables, and scale numerical data.

Example Data Preparation:

```
import pandas as pd

from sklearn.model_selection import train_test_split

from sklearn.preprocessing import StandardScaler

from sklearn.preprocessing import LabelEncoder


# Load the dataset

data = pd.read_csv('iris.csv')


# Encode categorical labels

le = LabelEncoder()

data['species'] = le.fit_transform(data['species'])


# Split the dataset into features and target
```

```
X = data.drop('species', axis=1)

y = data['species']


# Split into training and test sets

X_train, X_test, y_train, y_test = train_test_split(X, y,
test_size=0.2, random_state=42)


# Standardize features

scaler = StandardScaler()

X_train_scaled = scaler.fit_transform(X_train)

X_test_scaled = scaler.transform(X_test)
```

Model Training

Training a classification model involves selecting an appropriate algorithm and optimizing it to correctly classify the training data.

Using Scikit-learn for Classification:

Scikit-learn is a popular library for machine learning in Python, providing various classification algorithms.

Example of Model Training:

```
from sklearn.ensemble import RandomForestClassifier


# Initialize the model
```

```python
model = RandomForestClassifier()


# Train the model
model.fit(X_train_scaled, y_train)
```

Model Evaluation

Evaluating a classification model's performance is crucial to ensure its accuracy and reliability. Common metrics include Accuracy, Precision, Recall, F1 Score, and Confusion Matrix.

Example of Model Evaluation:

```python
from sklearn.metrics import accuracy_score, precision_score, recall_score, f1_score, confusion_matrix


# Make predictions
y_pred = model.predict(X_test_scaled)


# Calculate evaluation metrics
accuracy = accuracy_score(y_test, y_pred)

precision = precision_score(y_test, y_pred, average='weighted')

recall = recall_score(y_test, y_pred, average='weighted')

f1 = f1_score(y_test, y_pred, average='weighted')
```

```python
conf_matrix = confusion_matrix(y_test, y_pred)
```

```python
print(f'Accuracy: {accuracy}, Precision: {precision}, Recall: {recall}, F1 Score: {f1}')
```

```python
print(f'Confusion Matrix:\n{conf_matrix}')
```

Model Deployment with Azure ML

Deploying a classification model using Azure ML allows it to be accessed via an API endpoint, enabling real-time predictions.

Steps for Deployment:

1. **Model Registration**: Register the trained model in Azure ML workspace.

2. **Inference Configuration**: Define the environment and scoring script for the model.

3. **Deployment**: Deploy the model to a compute target such as Azure Container Instances (ACI) or Azure Kubernetes Service (AKS).

Example of Model Deployment:

```python
from azureml.core import Workspace, Model

from azureml.core.webservice import AciWebservice, Webservice

from azureml.core.model import InferenceConfig


# Connect to the workspace
```

```python
ws = Workspace.from_config()

# Register the model
model = Model.register(workspace=ws,
            model_name='classification_model',

model_path='outputs/classification_model.pkl')

# Define the inference configuration
inference_config                                    =
InferenceConfig(entry_script='score.py',
environment=env)

# Define the deployment configuration
deployment_config                                   =
AciWebservice.deploy_configuration(cpu_cores=1,
memory_gb=1)

# Deploy the model
service = Model.deploy(workspace=ws,
            name='classification-service',
            models=[model],
            inference_config=inference_config,
```

```
                deployment_config=deployment_config)
```

service.wait_for_deployment(show_output=True)

Monitoring and Managing the Deployed Model

Monitoring the deployed classification model ensures it maintains high performance and reliability. Azure ML provides tools for managing and tracking deployed models.

Monitoring Tools:

- **Azure ML Dashboard**: Visualize performance metrics and logs.

- **Application Insights**: Provides detailed telemetry data, such as response times and errors.

10. Neural Networks in Azure Machine Learning

Neural networks have revolutionized the field of artificial intelligence (AI) by enabling machines to learn and make decisions in a manner similar to the human brain. With the integration of Azure Machine Learning (Azure ML), creating, training, and deploying neural network models becomes an efficient and scalable process. This chapter explores the concepts, tools, and best practices for working with neural networks in Azure ML.

Overview of Neural Networks

Neural networks are composed of layers of interconnected nodes (or neurons) that process and transform data. Key components of neural networks include:

1. Input Layer: Accepts the input data.

2. Hidden Layers: Perform computations to extract features or patterns.

3. Output Layer: Produces predictions or classifications.

4. Activation Functions: Introduce non-linearity into the model, enabling it to learn complex patterns.

5. Weights and Biases: Parameters adjusted during training to minimize the error between predicted and actual outputs.

Common Types of Neural Networks

1. Feedforward Neural Networks (FNNs): Basic architecture for pattern recognition tasks.

2. Convolutional Neural Networks (CNNs): Specialized for image and spatial data analysis.

3. Recurrent Neural Networks (RNNs): Designed for sequential data like time series or text.

4. Transformers: State-of-the-art architecture for natural language processing tasks.

Setting Up Azure Machine Learning Workspace

To begin working with neural networks in Azure ML, set up your workspace by following these steps:

1. **Create an Azure ML Workspace:**

   o Go to the Azure Portal and create a new Azure ML workspace.

   o Configure the workspace with necessary compute and storage resources.

2. **Install Required SDKs:**

   pip install azureml-sdk

3. **Initialize the Workspace in Code:**

from azureml.core import Workspace

```python
ws = Workspace.from_config()

print(f"Workspace loaded: {ws.name}")
```

Building a Neural Network

Using PyTorch and TensorFlow in Azure ML

Azure ML supports popular deep learning frameworks like PyTorch and TensorFlow. Here is an example of building and training a simple neural network using PyTorch:

Define the Model:

```python
import torch

import torch.nn as nn

import torch.optim as optim


class SimpleN(n.Module):
    def __init__(self):
        super(SimpleN, self).__init__()
        self.fc1 = n.Linear(28*28, 128)
        self.relu = n.ReLU()
        self.fc2 = n.Linear(128, 10)

    def forward(self, x):
```

```python
        x = x.view(-1, 28*28)
        x = self.relu(self.fc1(x))
        x = self.fc2(x)
        return x


model = SimpleNN()
```

Train the Model:

```python
criterion = n.CrossEntropyLoss()
optimizer    =    optim.Adam(model.parameters(),
lr=0.001)


# Training loop
for epoch in range(epochs):
    for images, labels in train_loader:
        optimizer.zero_grad()
        outputs = model(images)
        loss = criterion(outputs, labels)
        loss.backward()
    optimizer.step()
```

Save the Model:

```python
        torch.save(model.state_dict(), "model.pth")
```

Registering and Deploying the Model

Register the Model in Azure ML:

```python
from azureml.core import Model

model = Model.register(workspace=ws,
                       model_path="model.pth",
                       model_name="simple_n_model")
print(f"Model registered: {model.name}")
```

Deploy the Model as a Web Service:

```python
from azureml.core.model import InferenceConfig
from azureml.core.webservice import AciWebservice

inference_config = InferenceConfig(entry_script="score.py",
environment=myenv)

deployment_config = AciWebservice.deploy_configuration(cpu_cores=1,
memory_gb=1)

service = Model.deploy(workspace=ws,
                       name="simple-n-service",
                       models=[model],
```

```
                inference_config=inference_config,

deployment_config=deployment_config)

service.wait_for_deployment(show_output=True)

print(f"Service state: {service.state}")
```

Test the Deployment:

```
import requests


data = {"data": [input_data]}

response    =    requests.post(service.scoring_uri,
json=data)

print(response.json())
```

Monitoring and Scaling Neural Networks

Azure ML provides capabilities to monitor and scale your deployed neural network:

1. Monitor Performance:

   o Use Azure Application Insights to monitor metrics like request latencies and errors.

2. Auto-Scale Resources:

   Configure Azure Kubernetes Service (AKS) to scale based on workload demands.

11. Embeddings in Azure Machine Learning

Embeddings are a powerful representation mechanism that converts high-dimensional data into lower-dimensional vector spaces while preserving semantic relationships. Widely used in natural language processing (NLP), recommendation systems, and other machine learning tasks, embeddings are instrumental for making sense of complex and unstructured data. In Azure Machine Learning (Azure ML), embeddings can be created, trained, and deployed with seamless integration.

Understanding Embeddings

Embeddings transform data points, such as words, sentences, or users, into dense vectors of continuous values. These vectors represent the relationships between the data points in a meaningful way, enabling machine learning models to perform efficiently on downstream tasks.

Key Characteristics of Embeddings

- Dimensionality Reduction: Embeddings reduce high-dimensional data to fewer dimensions, facilitating faster computations.

- Semantic Representation: Data points with similar meanings have vectors that are closer in the embedding space.

- Reusability: Once trained, embeddings can be reused across different tasks and models.

Common Applications

1. Text Embeddings: Word2Vec, GloVe, FastText, and transformer-based embeddings like BERT.

2. Graph Embeddings: Represent nodes and edges in a graph for link prediction or graph classification.

3. Recommendation Systems: Embeddings of users and items to predict preferences.

Creating Embeddings in Azure ML

Step 1: Preparing the Dataset

Data preprocessing is critical for building effective embeddings. For text data, this involves tokenization, lowercasing, and removal of stop words or punctuation.

from sklearn.model_selection import train_test_split

Example dataset

sentences = ["The quick brown fox", "jumps over the lazy dog", "Azure ML is great for AI"]

labels = [0, 1, 0]

Split data

```
train_texts,    test_texts,    train_labels,    test_labels    =
train_test_split(sentences, labels, test_size=0.2)
```

Step 2: Choosing an Embedding Model

Azure ML supports both custom embeddings and pretrained models. For text data, transformer models like BERT or GPT-3 are common choices. Here's an example with Hugging Face Transformers:

```
from transformers import AutoTokenizer, AutoModel


# Load tokenizer and model

model_name = "bert-base-uncased"

tokenizer                                          =
AutoTokenizer.from_pretrained(model_name)

model = AutoModel.from_pretrained(model_name)


# Tokenize input text

inputs    =    tokenizer(["Azure    ML    Embeddings"],
return_tensors="pt", padding=True, truncation=True)

embeddings = model(**inputs).last_hidden_state
```

Step 3: Training Custom Embeddings

For domain-specific tasks, fine-tuning pretrained models can yield better results. Use Azure ML's Compute Cluster for efficient training:

```
from azureml.core import ScriptRunConfig, Experiment
```

```python
from azureml.core.compute import ComputeTarget

# Define training script configuration
script_config                                    =
ScriptRunConfig(source_directory="./src",

                script="train_embeddings.py",

                compute_target="gpu-cluster")

# Start experiment
experiment        =        Experiment(workspace=ws,
name="embedding_training")
run = experiment.submit(script_config)
run.wait_for_completion(show_output=True)
```

Deploying Embeddings

Registering the Embedding Model

```python
from azureml.core.model import Model


model = Model.register(workspace=ws,

model_path="outputs/embedding_model",

                model_name="embedding_model")
print(f"Model registered: {model.name}")
```

Creating a Scoring Script

The scoring script defines how to preprocess input data and generate embeddings for inference:

```python
# score.py

import torch

from transformers import AutoTokenizer, AutoModel


def init():
    global model, tokenizer
    model_name = "bert-base-uncased"
    tokenizer = AutoTokenizer.from_pretrained(model_name)
    model = AutoModel.from_pretrained(model_name)


def run(data):
    inputs = tokenizer(data["text"], return_tensors="pt", padding=True, truncation=True)
    embeddings = model(**inputs).last_hidden_state
    return embeddings.detach().numpy().tolist()
```

Deploying as a Web Service

```python
from azureml.core.webservice import AciWebservice

from azureml.core.model import InferenceConfig
```

```python
# Configure inference

inference_config                              =
InferenceConfig(entry_script="score.py",
environment=myenv)

deployment_config                             =
AciWebservice.deploy_configuration(cpu_cores=1,
memory_gb=2)


# Deploy service

service = Model.deploy(workspace=ws,

                name="embedding-service",

                models=[model],

                inference_config=inference_config,

                deployment_config=deployment_config)

service.wait_for_deployment(show_output=True)
```

12. Large Language Models in Azure Machine Learning

Large Language Models (LLMs) are advanced AI systems trained on vast amounts of text data to perform a wide range of natural language processing (NLP) tasks. With capabilities such as text generation, summarization, translation, and code understanding, LLMs like GPT, BERT, and their derivatives have transformed the AI landscape. Azure Machine Learning provides a comprehensive platform to build, fine-tune, and deploy LLMs efficiently.

Understanding Large Language Models

LLMs are trained on massive datasets containing text from diverse sources, enabling them to:

- Understand Context: Analyze and interpret nuanced meanings in text.

- Generate Content: Produce coherent and contextually relevant text outputs.

- Adapt to Tasks: Perform specific tasks such as answering questions, writing summaries, and more.

Common Use Cases of LLMs

1. Content Creation: Generate articles, blogs, and creative writing.

2. Customer Support: Provide intelligent, automated responses to user queries.

3. Coding Assistance: Auto-complete code, identify bugs, and generate documentation.

4. Language Translation: Translate between multiple languages with high accuracy.

5. Knowledge Management: Summarize documents and extract insights from large text corpora.

Setting Up an LLM Workflow in Azure ML

Step 1: Selecting an LLM

Azure ML supports integrating pretrained LLMs from platforms like Hugging Face, OpenAI, and custom models. OpenAI models, including GPT series, can be accessed directly via Azure OpenAI Service.

```
from azure.ai.openai import OpenAIClient

from azure.identity import DefaultAzureCredential


# Authenticate and create a client

credential = DefaultAzureCredential()

client=OpenAIClient(endpoint="https://your-openai-endpoint.openai.azure.com/", credential=credential)

# List available models

models = client.list_models()

print([model.model_id for model in models])
```

Step 2: Fine-Tuning the Model

Fine-tuning helps adapt a generic LLM to domain-specific tasks or improve its performance on unique datasets.

Prepare the Dataset

Format the dataset appropriately (e.g., JSONL for OpenAI fine-tuning):

{"prompt": "Translate to French: Hello, how are you?\n", "completion": "Bonjour, comment ça va ?\n"}

Upload and Fine-Tune

```
response = client.begin_fine_tune(training_files=["dataset.jsonl"], model_id="gpt-3")

fine_tuned_model = response.result()

print(f"Fine-tuned model ID: {fine_tuned_model.model_id}")
```

Step 3: Deploying the Model

Deploying LLMs involves creating a scalable endpoint for real-time inference:

```
from azureml.core.model import InferenceConfig, Model

from azureml.core.webservice import AksWebservice


# Define inference configuration
```

```
inference_config                                    =
InferenceConfig(entry_script="score.py",
environment=myenv)
```

```
# AKS deployment
```

```
deployment_config                                  =
AksWebservice.deploy_configuration(cpu_cores=4,
memory_gb=16, enable_app_insights=True)
```

```
service=Model.deploy(workspace=ws,name="llm-
service",models=[model],
inference_config=inference_config,
deployment_config=deployment_config)
```

```
service.wait_for_deployment(show_output=True)
```

```
print(f"Service deployed at: {service.scoring_uri}")
```

Step 4: Interacting with the Model

Once deployed, interact with the model using HTTP requests or SDKs:

```
import requests
```

```
data = {"prompt": "Write a poem about Azure ML.",
"max_tokens": 100}
```

```
response = requests.post(service.scoring_uri, json=data)
```

```
print(response.json())
```

13. AutoML in Azure Machine Learning

Automated Machine Learning (AutoML) in Azure Machine Learning (Azure ML) democratizes the creation of sophisticated machine learning models by automating repetitive tasks like data preprocessing, algorithm selection, and hyperparameter optimization. It enables data scientists and developers to achieve state-of-the-art performance without extensive expertise in machine learning.

Introduction to AutoML

AutoML automates the end-to-end process of applying machine learning to real-world problems. The core components of AutoML include:

- Data Preparation: Ensures the dataset is clean, normalized, and ready for analysis.

- Model Selection: Identifies the best algorithms for a given task.

- Hyperparameter Tuning: Optimizes the model's parameters for improved accuracy.

- Evaluation: Compares models using metrics like accuracy, precision, and recall.

Azure ML's AutoML capabilities cater to classification, regression, time-series forecasting, and natural language processing tasks.

Setting Up AutoML in Azure Machine Learning

Step 1: Prerequisites

1. Azure Account: Set up a free or paid Azure account.

2. Azure ML Workspace: Create a workspace in Azure Portal.

3. Install SDK: Ensure you have the Azure ML SDK installed:

   pip install azureml-sdk

4. Compute Target: Create a compute cluster for running AutoML experiments.

Step 2: Prepare Your Dataset

Upload your dataset to Azure Blob Storage or the datastore associated with your workspace. Ensure the dataset is structured correctly, with clear feature columns and target labels.

from azureml.core import Workspace, Dataset

ws = Workspace.from_config()

datastore = ws.get_default_datastore()

Upload the dataset

datastore.upload(src_dir='data/', target_path='automl_data/', overwrite=True)

Register the dataset

```
dataset                                    =
Dataset.Tabular.from_delimited_files(path=(datastore,
'automl_data/data.csv'))
```

Step 3: Configure AutoML

Define the AutoML configuration for your specific task:

```
from azureml.train.automl import AutoMLConfig


automl_config = AutoMLConfig(

    task="classification",    # Options: "classification",
"regression", "forecasting"

    training_data=dataset,

    label_column_name="target",   # Replace with your
target column

    primary_metric="accuracy",  # Select metric relevant to
your task

    compute_target="gpu-cluster",    # Name of your
compute cluster

    experiment_timeout_minutes=60,

    enable_early_stopping=True,

    n_cross_validations=5
)
```

Step 4: Run the Experiment

Submit the AutoML experiment and monitor its progress:

```python
from azureml.core.experiment import Experiment


experiment = Experiment(ws, "automl_classification")

run=experiment.submit(automl_config,
show_output=True)
```

Step 5: Retrieve the Best Model

Once the experiment completes, retrieve the best model:

```python
best_run, fitted_model = run.get_output()

print(f"Best model: {fitted_model}")
```

Deploying the Best Model

Register the Model

```python
from azureml.core.model import Model


model=Model.register(workspace=ws,
model_name="best_automl_model",
model_path=fitted_model)
```

Deploy the Model

Deploy the model to an endpoint using Azure Container Instances (ACI):

```python
from azureml.core.webservice import AciWebservice

from azureml.core.model import InferenceConfig
```

```python
inference_config                                    =
InferenceConfig(entry_script="score.py",
environment=myenv)

aci_config                                          =
AciWebservice.deploy_configuration(cpu_cores=1,
memory_gb=1)


service=Model.deploy(workspace=ws,name="automl-
service",models=[model],
inference_config=inference_config,
deployment_config=aci_config)

service.wait_for_deployment(show_output=True)


print(f"Service URI: {service.scoring_uri}")
```

Test the Endpoint

Use the deployed endpoint for predictions:

```python
import requests


input_data = {"data": [[value1, value2, value3]]}    #
Replace with real data

response=requests.post(service.scoring_uri,
json=input_data)

print(response.json())
```

Advanced Features of Azure AutoML

Interpretability

Azure ML provides tools to interpret models created with AutoML, ensuring transparency and accountability:

from azureml.interpret import ExplanationClient

```
explanation_client                        =
ExplanationClient.from_run(best_run)

feature_importance=explanation_client.download_model
_explanation().get_feature_importance_dict()

print(feature_importance)
```

Hyperparameter Sweep

AutoML automatically performs hyperparameter tuning but allows custom sweep configurations for finer control:

From   azureml.train.hyperdrive   import GridParameterSampling, choice

```
param_sampling = GridParameterSampling({

    "learning_rate": choice(0.01, 0.1, 1),

    "batch_size": choice(16, 32, 64)
})
```

Time-Series Forecasting

For time-series tasks, specify the time column and the desired forecast horizon:

```
automl_config = AutoMLConfig(

    task="forecasting",

    training_data=dataset,

    label_column_name="target",

    time_column_name="timestamp",

    forecast_horizon=12

)
```

Best Practices for AutoML

1. Understand Your Data: Ensure the dataset is representative of the problem and free from biases.

2. Choose Appropriate Metrics: Select metrics that align with business objectives.

3. Iterate and Experiment: Run multiple AutoML experiments to find the most robust model.

4. Monitor Models in Production: Use Azure Monitor to track performance and detect drift.

14. Production ML Systems

Production Machine Learning (ML) systems are essential for transforming trained machine learning models into operational solutions that provide real-world value. While training and testing are significant steps in the ML pipeline, ensuring reliable and scalable production environments requires focused effort. Azure Machine Learning (Azure ML) offers comprehensive tools to support the deployment, monitoring, and maintenance of production ML systems.

Key Components of Production ML Systems

To operationalize machine learning, several components and considerations are crucial:

1. Model Deployment

- Ensures that trained models are accessible via APIs or other endpoints.

- Deployment options in Azure ML include:

  o Azure Kubernetes Service (AKS) for scalable deployments.

  o Azure Container Instances (ACI) for development and testing.

2. Inference Pipelines

- Handles prediction requests and returns results in real time or batch mode.

- Use Azure ML Pipelines to design workflows integrating preprocessing, inference, and postprocessing.

3. Scalability and Availability

- AKS allows dynamic scaling to handle fluctuating workloads.

- Leverage load balancers and geographic replication for high availability.

4. Model Monitoring and Management

- Track prediction performance, latency, and system health.

- Monitor model drift using Azure Monitor or integrate with third-party tools.

5. Continuous Integration and Continuous Deployment (CI/CD)

- Employ Azure DevOps or GitHub Actions to automate testing and deployment workflows.

- Ensure automated model retraining pipelines adapt to new data.

Deploying ML Models to Production

The process involves several steps to ensure the model meets production requirements:

Step 1: Register the Model

After training, register the best model in Azure ML workspace to track its versioning:

```python
from azureml.core import Model


model = Model.register(
    workspace=ws,
    model_name="production_model",
    model_path="outputs/model.pkl"
)
```

Step 2: Define the Inference Environment

Create an inference configuration, specifying the scoring script and dependencies:

```python
from azureml.core.model import InferenceConfig


inference_config = InferenceConfig(
    entry_script="score.py",
    environment=myenv    # Predefined Azure ML Environment
)
```

Step 3: Deploy the Model

Choose the appropriate deployment target (e.g., ACI or AKS):

```python
from azureml.core.webservice import AciWebservice

deployment_config                                    =
AciWebservice.deploy_configuration(
    cpu_cores=1,
    memory_gb=1
)


service = Model.deploy(
    workspace=ws,
    name="ml-service",
    models=[model],
    inference_config=inference_config,
    deployment_config=deployment_config
)
service.wait_for_deployment(show_output=True)
```

Step 4: Test the Endpoint

Ensure the deployed model returns correct and efficient results:

```python
import requests
```

```python
input_data = {"data": [[feature1, feature2, feature3]]}  # Replace with real input

response = requests.post(service.scoring_uri, json=input_data)

print(response.json())
```

Monitoring and Maintaining Production Models

1. Model Performance Monitoring

Regularly assess key performance metrics like accuracy and latency. Integrate Azure Monitor or Application Insights for:

- Tracking API response times.
- Analyzing resource utilization.

2. Model Drift Detection

Changes in data distribution over time, known as model drift, can degrade model performance:

- Automate retraining triggers using Azure ML pipelines and drift detection tools.

3. Versioning and Rollbacks

Maintain multiple versions of the model in Azure ML:

- Promote well-performing versions to production.
- Roll back if new deployments underperform.

4. Security and Compliance

- Use Azure Role-Based Access Control (RBAC) to secure deployments.

- Ensure compliance with industry standards (e.g., GDPR, HIPAA) via Azure Policy.

CI/CD Pipelines for ML

Azure DevOps and GitHub Actions facilitate seamless CI/CD for ML:

Step 1: Automate Testing and Validation

Implement automated pipelines to validate:

- Data quality.

- Model accuracy and consistency across versions.

Step 2: Build and Deploy Workflow

Define YAML pipelines for consistent and reproducible model deployments:

```
trigger:
- main


jobs:
- job: Deploy
  steps:
  - task: AzureMLDeploy@1
    inputs:
```

```
model: "production_model.pkl"
serviceName: "ml-service"
inferenceConfig: "score.py"
```

15. ML Fairness in Azure Machine Learning

Machine Learning (ML) fairness is a critical consideration in the development and deployment of ML systems to ensure that the models provide equitable outcomes for all user groups. In Azure Machine Learning (Azure ML), fairness is addressed through a set of tools and methodologies designed to identify, mitigate, and monitor biases in data and models.

Understanding ML Fairness

ML fairness focuses on reducing bias and ensuring that predictive models do not discriminate against individuals or groups based on sensitive attributes, such as race, gender, age, or socioeconomic status. This requires:

1. **Bias Detection**: Identifying data or model biases that result in unfair outcomes.

2. **Fairness Metrics**: Quantifying fairness through metrics such as disparate impact or equalized odds.

3. **Mitigation Strategies**: Addressing biases during data preprocessing, model training, and postprocessing.

4. **Continuous Monitoring**: Ensuring models maintain fairness in production environments.

Azure ML Tools for Fairness

Azure ML provides robust tools to analyze and improve model fairness:

1. Fairlearn

Fairlearn is an open-source Python library integrated into Azure ML for assessing and improving fairness. It provides:

- **Fairness Metrics**: Tools for calculating fairness metrics across different subgroups.

- **Mitigation Algorithms**: Methods for adjusting models to reduce bias.

2. Responsible AI Dashboard

The Responsible AI Dashboard integrates various fairness and interpretability tools to enable:

- Comprehensive assessment of fairness metrics.

- Visual inspection of disparities across groups.

- Generation of actionable insights for fairness improvement.

Implementing ML Fairness in Azure

Step 1: Install Required Libraries

Ensure you have Fairlearn and Azure ML installed:

pip install fairlearn azureml-sdk

Step 2: Evaluate Fairness Metrics

Load your model and dataset to calculate fairness metrics:

```python
from fairlearn.metrics import MetricFrame,
selection_rate, demographic_parity_difference

from sklearn.metrics import accuracy_score


# Example metrics
accuracy = accuracy_score(y_true, y_pred)
metric_frame = MetricFrame(
    metrics={"accuracy": accuracy, "selection_rate":
selection_rate},
    y_true=y_true,
    y_pred=y_pred,
    sensitive_features=sensitive_attribute
)


print("Overall Metrics:")
print(metric_frame.overall)
print("Metrics by Group:")
print(metric_frame.by_group)
```

Step 3: Mitigate Bias

Apply mitigation algorithms to reduce bias. For example, reweighting the dataset:

```python
from fairlearn.reductions import ExponentiatedGradient
```

```python
from fairlearn.reductions import DemographicParity


# Train a fair classifier

mitigator = ExponentiatedGradient(estimator=model,
constraints=DemographicParity())

mitigator.fit(X_train,                              y_train,
sensitive_features=sensitive_attribute)


# Generate predictions

y_pred_mitigated = mitigator.predict(X_test)
```

Step 4: Integrate with Responsible AI Dashboard

Use Azure's Responsible AI tools to visualize and understand fairness results:

```python
from             azureml.contrib.fairness         import
upload_dashboard_data


# Prepare and upload data to Azure

upload_dashboard_data(
    workspace=ws,
    dashboard_name="Fairness Dashboard",
    y_true=y_test,
    y_pred=y_pred,
```

```
    sensitive_features=sensitive_attribute
)
```

Key Fairness Metrics

Azure ML provides several fairness metrics to evaluate model behavior across sensitive groups:

- **Demographic Parity**: Ensures similar selection rates across groups.

- **Equalized Odds**: Checks equal error rates (false positives and false negatives).

- **Disparate Impact**: Measures ratio of outcomes between groups (e.g., hiring rate).

- **Treatment Equality**: Balances cost-related outcomes across groups.

Best Practices for Ensuring Fairness

1. **Understand the Domain**: Identify fairness requirements based on the specific use case and its impact.

2. **Use Diverse Datasets**: Ensure training data represents the full diversity of the target population.

3. **Measure Fairness Regularly**: Use metrics to continuously assess and address fairness concerns.

4. **Collaborate Across Teams**: Involve stakeholders, ethicists, and affected groups in the development process.

5. **Automate Monitoring**: Implement automated fairness checks for deployed models to identify drift and mitigate bias.

Ethical Considerations in ML Fairness

Fairness in ML extends beyond technical metrics to address broader ethical concerns. Key considerations include:

- **Transparency**: Ensure clear communication of how models make decisions.

- **Inclusivity**: Involve marginalized groups in the fairness evaluation process.

- **Accountability**: Assign responsibility for addressing fairness challenges at every stage of the ML lifecycle.

•

16. Troubleshooting for Common Issues in Azure Machine Learning Workflows

Azure Machine Learning (Azure ML) offers a rich platform for developing, training, deploying, and monitoring machine learning models. However, issues can arise during the workflow, particularly when dealing with resource configuration, data management, or deployment. This guide outlines common problems and solutions to help troubleshoot Azure ML workflows effectively.

General Troubleshooting Process

1. **Identify the Issue**: Understand what isn't working. Look for error messages and logs.

2. **Check Documentation**: Refer to Azure ML's official documentation for guidance on the error.

3. **Use Azure Portal**: Utilize Azure portal diagnostics to investigate issues in compute, storage, and deployed services.

4. **Consult Logs**: Review logs from Azure ML experiments, pipelines, and deployments for detailed error information.

Common Issues and Solutions

1. Environment Configuration

Problem: SDK Installation Errors

- **Symptoms**: Errors while installing or importing the Azure ML SDK.

- **Solution**:

  - Ensure you have the correct Python version (3.6 - 3.10).

  - Create a clean Python virtual environment:

    python -m venv myenv

    source myenv/bin/activate

    pip install azureml-sdk

  - Upgrade pip and check dependencies:

    pip install --upgrade pip setuptools

Problem: Environment Build Failures

- **Symptoms**: Environment build fails during pipeline or deployment.

- **Solution**:

  - Check the requirements.txt or conda.yaml file for missing or incompatible dependencies.

  - Debug locally by replicating the environment using Docker or Conda.

2. Compute and Resource Issues

Problem: Compute Cluster Creation Failure

- **Symptoms**: Errors during compute cluster setup.
- **Solution**:
    - Verify region availability for the VM size you're trying to create.
    - Ensure quota limits are sufficient for the requested resources. Update quotas via the Azure Portal if needed.
    - Check your Azure subscription permissions for resource creation.

Problem: Compute Node Unavailability

- **Symptoms**: Jobs remain queued or fail to start.
- **Solution**:
    - Ensure compute cluster nodes are not deallocated. Restart nodes if necessary.
    - Check for overutilization; scale the cluster to increase capacity.

---

3. Experiment and Model Training Issues

Problem: Experiment Run Fails

- **Symptoms**: Error messages during execution or missing output.

- **Solution**:

  - Use the RunDetails widget in Jupyter or Azure Studio to inspect logs.

  - Check for dataset access permissions and format compatibility.

Problem: Long Execution Time

- **Symptoms**: Experiments take significantly longer than expected.

- **Solution**:

  - Use GPU-accelerated compute if applicable.

  - Optimize training code for parallelization and efficient resource usage.

  - Profile your script for bottlenecks.

---

4. Data Management Problems

Problem: Dataset Registration Errors

- **Symptoms**: Unable to register datasets in Azure ML.

- **Solution**:

  - Ensure correct file paths and supported formats.

- Verify datastore connections and authentication credentials.

Problem: Data Access Issues in Remote Runs

- **Symptoms**: Experiment runs fail to access registered datasets.

- **Solution**:

  - Check datastore configurations and SAS token validity.

  - Ensure the compute environment has access to the same network or storage account.

---

5. Model Deployment Issues

Problem: Deployment Failure

- **Symptoms**: Errors during model deployment to ACI or AKS.

- **Solution**:

  - Validate the scoring script (entry_script) and model path during deployment.

  - Review deployment logs for errors in dependency resolution or script execution.

  - Ensure enough resources are allocated for the deployment.

Problem: Endpoint Unresponsive

- **Symptoms**: REST endpoint is unreachable or slow to respond.

- **Solution**:

  - Test the endpoint using Postman or requests in Python.

  - Check the health of the underlying container instances or nodes.

  - Ensure networking configurations (e.g., firewalls, VNET) allow access.

Problem: Prediction Errors

- **Symptoms**: Endpoint returns incorrect or unexpected results.

- **Solution**:

  - Verify input data formats match model expectations.

  - Use tools like Azure Monitor to analyze logs and telemetry for issues in the scoring function.

---

6. Pipelines and Scheduling Issues

Problem: Pipeline Execution Failure

- **Symptoms**: Pipelines do not complete or fail at specific steps.

- **Solution**:

- o Examine logs for failed steps and debug individual components.

- o Validate dataset versions and compute targets.

Problem: Scheduling Errors

- **Symptoms**: Scheduled pipelines fail or run unexpectedly.

- **Solution**:

  - o Ensure the triggering mechanism (manual or automated) is correctly configured.

  - o Check pipeline permissions and service principal roles for scheduler access.

---

7. Monitoring and Maintenance Issues

Problem: Drift Detection Failure

- **Symptoms**: Model monitoring tools do not detect drift.

- **Solution**:

  - o Verify the dataset version and features monitored for drift.

  - o Ensure telemetry collection is enabled for deployed endpoints.

Problem: Metrics Logging Issues

- **Symptoms**: Metrics do not appear in Azure Monitor.

- **Solution**:

  - Validate integration with Azure Monitor or Application Insights.

  - Check network configurations for blocked telemetry data flow.

17. Real-World Case Studies: Successful Implementations of Azure Machine Learning Across Industries

Azure Machine Learning (Azure ML) has emerged as a versatile platform, empowering organizations across industries to harness the potential of artificial intelligence and machine learning. This chapter showcases real-world case studies demonstrating the successful deployment of Azure ML for solving critical business challenges, driving innovation, and delivering measurable impact.

Healthcare: Personalized Cancer Treatment at Cambrian BioPharma

Problem

Cambrian BioPharma sought to develop personalized cancer treatments by identifying the most effective drug combinations for individual patients. The challenge lay in processing vast amounts of genomic and clinical data to deliver precise and actionable insights.

Solution

Using Azure ML, Cambrian BioPharma implemented:

- **Data Integration Pipelines**: Leveraging Azure Data Factory and Azure ML to integrate genomic, imaging, and clinical datasets.

- **Deep Learning Models**: Training neural networks for predicting drug efficacy based on patient-specific biomarkers.

- **Explainable AI**: Using Fairlearn to ensure transparency and fairness in treatment recommendations.

Outcome

- **Speed**: Reduced the time to analyze patient data from weeks to hours.

- **Accuracy**: Increased prediction accuracy for effective drug combinations by 30%.

- **Scalability**: Scaled the model to handle data for 10,000+ patients per month.

Retail: Demand Forecasting for Contoso Retail Chain

Problem

Contoso, a leading retail chain, faced challenges in inventory management due to inaccurate demand forecasting, leading to overstocking or understocking.

Solution

The company deployed Azure ML to build an automated demand forecasting system:

- **Time-Series Forecasting**: Using Azure AutoML's forecasting capabilities to predict product demand.

- **Model Management**: Leveraging Azure ML's model registry to version and track deployed models.

- **Integration with Operations**: Deploying the model to an Azure Kubernetes Service (AKS) endpoint for real-time decision-making.

Outcome

- **Inventory Optimization**: Reduced overstocking by 20% and understocking by 15%.

- **Operational Efficiency**: Increased forecasting accuracy by 35%, improving overall supply chain efficiency.

- **Cost Savings**: Saved millions in storage and operational costs annually.

Manufacturing: Predictive Maintenance for Global Tech

Problem

Global Tech, a multinational manufacturing firm, aimed to reduce downtime caused by unexpected equipment failures.

Solution

Azure ML enabled the company to:

- **Sensor Data Analytics**: Integrate IoT Hub and Azure ML to analyze sensor data from equipment.

- **Predictive Models**: Build and deploy machine learning models to predict failures before they occur.

- **Visualization**: Use Power BI to present actionable insights to engineers and decision-makers.

Outcome

- **Uptime Increase**: Reduced equipment downtime by 40%.

- **Cost Reduction**: Saved $5 million annually by preventing failures and optimizing maintenance schedules.

- **Proactive Decision-Making**: Empowered engineers with real-time failure predictions and insights.

Financial Services: Fraud Detection at Contoso Bank

Problem

Contoso Bank struggled with identifying and mitigating fraudulent transactions in real-time without impacting customer experience.

Solution

Azure ML played a critical role in implementing a robust fraud detection system:

- **Real-Time Analysis**: Building pipelines to process transactional data in real time using Azure Stream Analytics.

- **Advanced Models**: Training gradient-boosted tree models on Azure ML to classify fraudulent transactions.

- **Model Monitoring**: Deploying Azure Monitor to track model performance and retrain models as required.

Outcome

- **Fraud Mitigation**: Reduced fraud loss by 45%.

- **Customer Trust**: Improved transaction approval rates without false positives.

- **Scalability**: Supported millions of transactions per minute with minimal latency.

Energy: Smart Grid Optimization at EnergyPlus

Problem

EnergyPlus, a renewable energy provider, aimed to optimize grid operations by balancing demand and renewable energy supply.

Solution

Using Azure ML, the company implemented a smart grid optimization system:

- **Demand Forecasting**: Utilizing time-series models to predict energy demand across regions.

- **Supply Optimization**: Integrating solar and wind energy forecasts to optimize grid dispatch.

- **Real-Time Deployment**: Deploying models on edge devices for localized grid management.

Outcome

- **Efficiency Gains**: Improved grid efficiency by 25%.

- **Sustainability**: Reduced reliance on fossil fuels by 40%.

- **Cost Savings**: Lowered operational costs by $2 million annually.

Logistics: Route Optimization for Global Freight

Problem

Global Freight, a logistics giant, faced challenges in minimizing delivery times and fuel costs across its fleet.

Solution

The company implemented Azure ML to optimize routing:

- **Route Planning Models**: Developing machine learning models to identify the shortest and most fuel-efficient routes.

- **Dynamic Updates**: Incorporating real-time traffic data using Azure Maps and APIs.

- **Integration**: Deploying the solution through Azure Functions for seamless integration with fleet management systems.

Outcome

- **Faster Deliveries**: Reduced average delivery times by 15%.

- **Fuel Savings**: Decreased fuel consumption by 10%, contributing to sustainability goals.

- **Enhanced Customer Satisfaction**: Improved delivery predictability and transparency.

www.ingramcontent.com/pod-product-compliance
Lightning Source LLC
La Vergne TN
LVHW051704050326
832903LV00032B/4002